THE NEST

Franz Xaver Kroetz

in a new translation by
Conor McPherson

1–22 October 2016, Lyric Theatre, Belfast
28 October–26 November 2016, Young Vic, London

A Lyric Theatre, Belfast and Young Vic co-production

Martha	Caoilfhionn Dunne
Kurt	Laurence Kinlan

Author	Franz Xaver Kroetz
Translated by	Conor McPherson
Director	Ian Rickson
Set and Costume Designer	Alyson Cummins
Lighting Designer	Zia Holly
Sound Designer	Gregory Clarke
Original score composed by	PJ Harvey
Performed by	PJ Harvey and James Johnston
Score engineered by	Adam 'Cecil' Bartlett and recorded in London
Movement Director	Andrew Dawson
Assistant Director	Rhiann Jeffrey

Production Managers	Alan McCracken
	Scott Handley
Company Stage Manager	Kate Miller
Stage Manager	Jade Nagi
Deputy Stage Manager	Alicia White
Technical Manager	Keith Ginty
Technician (Lyric Theatre)	Ian Vennard
Lighting Technician (Young Vic)	Jess Glaisher
Wardrobe Supervisor	Enda Kenny
Costume Assistant	Fay Bescoby

The Lyric Theatre's licence to present Franz Xaver Kroetz's play *The Nest* in a co-production with the Young Vic Theatre, London is granted by Rosica Colin Limited, London, and on Conor McPherson's behalf by Curtis Brown, London.

The producers would like to extend their thanks to Nica Burns and Nimax Theatres Limited for their generous support of this production.

Actors

Caoilfhionn Dunne plays Martha, making her Lyric Theatre and Young Vic debut. Her previous theatre credits include: Conor McPherson's *The Night Alive* and *Fathers and Sons* (Donmar Warehouse); *Wild* (Hampstead); *Forever Yours, Mary-Lou* (Ustinov, Bath); *Our Country's Good, The Veil* (National Theatre); *King Lear, Christ Deliver Us!, The Last Days of a Reluctant Tyrant* (Abbey); *Pineapple, 10 Dates with Mad Mary* (Calipo); *Plasticine* (Corcadorca); *La Dispute* (Peacock); *The Playboy of the Western World* (Druid USA tour); *The Sanctuary Lamp* (b*spoke Theatre Company); *Bent* (Smock Alley); *Macbeth* (Siren Prods) and *Caligula* (Rough Magic Seeds III; nominated for Best Actress at the Dublin Fringe Festival Awards). Her film credits include: *In View, Traders, Wrath of the Titans, Walls, Corduroy.* For television, credits include: *Love/Hate III/IV/V, Vexed II, Little White Lie.*

Laurence Kinlan plays Kurt, making his Young Vic debut. His theatre credits include: *The Cripple of Inishmaan* (Druid); *The Playboy of the Western World, The Plough and the Stars* (Abbey); *Poor Beast in the Rain, The Threepenny Opera* (Gate); *Saved* (Peacock) and *The Night Alive* (Gaiety Theatre and Lyric Theatre Belfast). Film credits include: *Ned Kelly, Veronica Guerin, Intermission, Angela's Ashes, Saltwater, Everlasting Piece, Last Days in Dublin, On The Nose, Breakfast on Pluto, The Guard* and *Soft Sand, Blue Sea.* Television credits include: *Love/Hate* and *Charlie.*

Creative Team

FRANZ XAVER KROETZ – Author
Franz Xaver Kroetz is a German author, playwright, actor and director.
His plays include: *Through the Leaves, Mensch Meier* (Tom Fool), *The Nest, Das Ende der Paarung, Game Crossing, Stubborn, Working at Home* and *Request Programme*. For television, credits include: *Kir Royale*. For radio, his work includes: *Reise ins Glück/Awayday*. For opera, his work includes: *Stallerhof*, based on his play of the same name and which premiered at the first Munich Biennale in 1988 (composer Gerd Kühr).

CONOR McPHERSON – Translation
Conor McPherson was born in Dublin in 1971. He was educated at University College Dublin where he began to write and direct. His plays include *Rum & Vodka, The Good Thief, This Lime Tree Bower, St. Nicholas, The Weir*, which won an Olivier Award for Best Play, *Dublin Carol, Port Authority, Shining City*, nominated for a Tony Award for Best Play, *The Seafarer*, nominated for a Tony, Olivier and Evening Standard Award for Best Play, *The Veil* and *The Night Alive*, which won the New York Drama Critics' Circle Award for Best Play and was nominated for an Olivier Award for Best Play.

IAN RICKSON – Director
Ian Rickson makes his Lyric Theatre debut, and returns to the Young Vic after directing *Hamlet* in 2011. His theatre credits include: *Jerusalem* (Royal Court, West End and Broadway), which won a Tony, Olivier and Evening Standard Award; *The Children's Hour, Betrayal, Old Times* (West End); *Hedda Gabler* (Broadway); *Parlour Song* (Almeida); *The Hothouse, The Red Lion, Evening at the Talkhouse* (National Theatre); *The River* (Royal Court and Broadway). He was Artistic Director of the Royal Court from 1997–2007 where his credits include: *The Weir,* nominated for an Olivier Award, *The Seagull* (Broadway), *Krapp's Last Tape, Mouth to Mouth* (West End), *The Alice Trilogy* and *Mojo* (revived in the West End).

ALYSON CUMMINS – Set and Costume Designer
Alyson Cummins' previous stage design includes: *Quietly* (The Irish Rep New York & The Public Theater); *FABRIC* UK tour (TREMers); *Macbeth* (Iford Arts); *This Lime Tree Bower* (Project Arts Centre); *The Lighthouse* (Linbury Studio, Royal Opera House); *The Night Alive* (Dublin Theatre Festival, Lyric Belfast); *I Know All the Secrets in My World* (Tiata Fahodzi); *Pentecost* (Lyric Belfast – winner best set design Irish Times Theatre Awards 2015); *Heartbreak House, The Risen People, Quietly, Perve, No Escape* (Abbey); *Be Infants in Evil* (Druid); *Summertime* (Tinderbox); *It's a Family Affair* (Sherman Cymru); *Mixed Marriage* (Lyric Belfast); *Before it Rains* (Bristol Old Vic and Sherman Cymru); *Pornography* (Waking Exploits); *Pigeon* (Carpet Theatre); *Ruben Guthri* (Iron Bark); *How the World Began* (Arcola, Tom Atkins and Out of Joint); *Hamlet* (Second Age); *The Trailer of Bridget Dinnigan* (ITM); *Colleen Bawn* (Project/Civic/Bedrock); *Off Plan*, Project (RAW); *Serious Money* and *Dying City* (Rough Magic Seeds); *The Trials of Brother Jero; Through a Film Darkly* (Arambe); *Ya Get Me* (Old Vic Education Department).

ZIA HOLLY – Lighting Designer

Zia Holly's Lyric Theatre credits: *The Night Alive* (Lyric Theatre and Dublin Theatre Festival). Other theatre credits include: *FABRIC* (Robin Rayner and TREMers/Scotsman Fringe First Award winner 2016); *Northern Star, Enjoy, Unspoken, Anna Belle Eema, Assassins, Way to Heaven* (Rough Magic); *Inhabitance, Broadening* (nominated for Best Design at the Dublin Absolut Fringe Awards 2012) (Glass Doll); *They Called Her Vivaldi, The True Story of Hansel and Gretel* (Theatre Lovett); *East of Berlin* (Brinkmanship Theatre); *The Dead* (Dublin Theatre Festival); *Before Monsters Were Made, Reckoners* (15th Oak); *East of Berlin, Northern Star* (The Lir Academy); *On the Wire* (Wildebeest Theatre, nominated for Best Production at the Irish Times Theatre Awards 2015); *The Last 5 Years* (Trees Rd Productions); *The Separation* (Pixilated); *Flesh and Blood Women* (Green Shoot Productions); *Turn Out the Lights* (Sounds Alive); *LAMBO, Clear The Air* (Underscore Productions); *HUMAN CHILD* (Collapsing Horse); *The Nutcracker, Romeo and Juliet* (Ballet Ireland).

GREGORY CLARKE – Sound Designer

Gregory's theatre credits include: *The Two Noble Kinsmen, All's Well That Ends Well, Coriolanus, The Merry Wives of Windsor, Tantalus, Cymbeline, A Midsummer Night's Dream* (Royal Shakespeare Company); *Medea, The Doctor's Dilemma, Misterman, Tristan & Yseult* (National Theatre); *The Truth, Dinner With Saddam, Assassins, Two Into One, The Lyons, Travels With My Aunt, Proof* (Menier Chocolate Factory); *Welcome Home Captain Fox!, My Night With Reg, Versailles, The Night Alive, A Voyage Around My Father, The Philanthropist* (Donmar Warehouse); *The Color Purple* (Broadway); *The Twits, The Ritual Slaughter of Gorge Mastromas* (Royal Court); *The Merchant of Venice, Cloud Nine* (Almeida); *Clarence Darrow, A Flea In Her Ear, National Anthems, Six Degrees of Separation* (The Old Vic); *Journey's End* (Duke of York's/New York, Drama Desk Award for Outstanding Sound Design); *Equus* (Gielgud/New York, Tony Award for Best Sound Design); *DruidMurphy, DruidShakespreare, Brigit, Bailegangaire, Waiting For Godot* (Druid Theatre); *The Night Alive, The Philanthropist, Pygmalion* (New York).

PJ HARVEY – Original Score

PJ Harvey has released nine critically acclaimed albums, been nominated for six Grammy Awards, and is the only artist to have been awarded the UK's prestigious Mercury Prize twice (for the albums *Stories from the City, Stories from the Sea* and *Let England Shake*). *The Hope Six Demolition Project*, released this April, reached #1 in the UK Album Charts. Her previous collaborations with director Ian Rickson include original scores for *Hedda Gabler* (American Airlines Theatre), Ophelia for *Hamlet* (Young Vic) and the 2014 production of *Electra* (Old Vic). Harvey has contributed original music to soundtracks including for Mark Cousins' *What's This Film Called Love?*, Tim Robbins' *The Cradle Will Rock*, Julian Schnabel's *Basquiat* and the BBC2 television series *Peaky Blinders*. PJ Harvey's first collection of poetry titled *The Hollow of the Hand*, in collaboration with photographer Seamus Murphy, was published by Bloomsbury in October 2015.

ANDREW DAWSON – Movement Director
Born in Sussex, UK, lives in London and Los Angeles. He studied dance with
Merce Cunningham, theatre with Phillipe Gaulier, Monika Pagneux, Jacques
Lecoq and The Feldenkrais Method. He created and performed the shows
Thunderbirds F.A.B., Space Panorama (Mime Theatre Project, 1984–1992)
Quatre Mains and *Absence & Presence.* Directing credits include *Wallace and
Gromit Alive on Stage, Amnesia Curiosa* (Rainpan 43)*; Pandora 88* (Fabrik
Potsdam) and *The Idiot Colony* (Redcape Theatre). Movement Director on
operas: *Dr. Atomic* and *The Pearl Fishers* (ENO & MET New York); *A
Midsummer Night's Dream* (Bristol Old Vic). With an arts award from
Wellcome Trust, he created *The Articulate Hand,* featured as three talks at
TEDMED and *The Russian Doctor,* Chekhov's Journey to Sakhalin Island.
Under commission from The Royal Opera House he created *Spirit of the Ring,*
Wagner's entire Ring Cycle in thirty minutes with little more than his hands
and a table for a stage.

RHIANN JEFFREY – Assistant Director
Rhiann Jeffrey has recently completed a year as a BBC Performing Arts
Fellow with Primecut Productions through which she directed her first
professional production *Mydidae* by Jack Thorne. Throughout this placement,
she also assisted Emma Jordan on a new version of *After Miss Julie* by Patrick
Marber and on *God of Carnage* by Yasmina Reza. Earlier this year Rhiann
directed the premiere of *Me, Here Me* by Jane Coyle. She graduated in Drama
from Queen's University in 2014, where she directed a number of plays
including: *Punk Rock* by Simon Stephens, *The Cracks in my Skin* by Phil
Porter, and *Her Naked Skin* by Rebecca Lenkiewicz. During her degree,
Rhiann assisted Kurt Taroff on *The Current Crisis* and was the assistant
director for Patsy Hughes, on Greenroom Productions' *After the Bell Jar.* She
also worked on *The Flying Dutchman* for NI Opera and for Field Day Theatre
Company on *A Particle of Dread*, directed by Nancy Meckler.

LYRIC
THEATRE

This production of *The Nest* encapsulates much of what the Lyric Theatre is about: bringing to life a pulsating piece of theatre; collaborating with a dynamic, like-minded producing partner; presenting the latest work from one of Ireland's leading playwrights; and bringing together a world-class director, an award-winning composer, two astonishingly talented young actors, and an exciting creative team. We are thrilled to be working with Conor McPherson once again following the success of *The Night Alive* last year, and delighted to be working with the Young Vic and Ian Rickson for the first time.

Over the past sixty-five years, the Lyric has established itself as Northern Ireland's leading producing theatre, premiering the works of playwrights such as Stewart Parker, Martin Lynch, Marie Jones and Christina Reid, and showcasing the talents of Northern Ireland's finest actors, including Adrian Dunbar, Conleth Hill, Stella McCusker, Ciarán Hinds, Frances Tomelty and the Theatre's patron, Liam Neeson.

The Lyric's mission is to produce high-quality professional theatre that is alive to the complex cultural experience and diverse traditions of Northern Ireland, and to use the power of live theatre to inspire, engage, educate and empower.

From first rehearsal to final curtain, the shows we create are truly indigenous products of Northern Ireland. Putting local issues and local characters centre stage is what the Lyric does best. Our shows are relevant to local audiences and revealing to visitors to the city. And a very important part of the Lyric Theatre's strategy is to tour as widely as possible, to give audiences outside Northern Ireland an insight into our culture and to the work of the Lyric.

Officially opened in May 2011 by Brian Friel, the Lyric's new home on the banks of Belfast's River Lagan, on the site of the previous theatre, is a landmark £18.1m building that signals the continued regeneration of the city and is a catalyst for real progress in arts infrastructure for artists and audiences alike.

Designed by O'Donnell + Tuomey, and built in a stunning blend of Belfast brick, glass, steel, concrete and Iroko timber, the new theatre is alive and dramatic at all times. Spacious lobbies and bars overlooking the river, and two beautiful auditoria with an exciting artistic programme, makes the Lyric a thriving social hub, creative learning space and a real attraction for visitors to the city.

LYRIC THEATRE STAFF

Board of Directors
Sir Bruce Robinson
(Chairman)
Stephen Douds (Vice Chair)
Phil Cheevers
Nicky Dunn
Henry Elvin
Patricia McBride
Sid McDowell
Dr Mark Phelan

Patron
Liam Neeson OBE
Artist in Residence
Duke Special

Executive Producer
Jimmy Fay
Apprentice Producer
Bronagh McFeely
Chief Operating Officer
Ciaran McAuley
Literary Manager
Rebecca Mairs

**Head of Marketing and
Communications**
Simon Goldrick
Marketing Manager
Aisling McKenna
Marketing Officer
Aiveen Kelly

Company Stage Manager
Kate Miller
Deputy Stage Managers
Tracey Lindsay
Aimee Yates
Assistant Stage Managers
Louise Bryans
Stephen Dix

Production Manager
Alan McCracken
Technical Manager
Keith Ginty
Technicians
Damian Cox
Ian Vennard
Tighearnan O'Neill

Wardrobe Supervisor
Enda Kenny
Wardrobe Assistant
Erin Charteris

Administration Manager
Clare Gault
Administration Assistant
Cat Rice

Head of Finance
Deirdre Ferguson
Finance Manager
Micheal Meegan

Housekeeping
Debbie Duff
Amanda Richards
Samantha Walker

Head of Creative Learning
Philip Crawford
**Creative Learning
Co-Ordinator**
Niki Doherty
Creative Learning Assistant
Pauline McKay
Creative Learning Intern
Erin Hoey

Customer Service Manager
Ciara McCann
Duty Managers
Rebecca Cooney
Marina Hampton
Barry Leonard
Ashlene McGurk

Maitre D'
Cliff Hylands
Chef
Ross McMullan

Box Office Supervisor
Emily White
**Box Office Deputy
Supervisor**
Paul McCaffrey

**Customer Service and
Box Office Staff**
Pamela Armstrong
Lauren Bailey
Luke Bannon
Michael Bingham
Carla Bryson
Paula Ruth Carson-Lewis
Rebecca Cooney
Hannah Conlon
Emmett Costello
Stephen Coulter
Andrew Cowan
Ellison Craig

Gary Crossan
Alacoque Davey
Catherine Davison
Amanda Doherty
Scott English
Darren Franklin
Catriona Grant
Chris Grant
Adele Gribbon
Peter Hackett
Simon Hall
Laura Hamill
Marina Hampton
David Hanna
Cathal Henry
Teresa Hill
Erin Hoey
Aaron Hughes
Niamh Johnson
Megan Keenan
Gerard Kelly
Julie Lamberton
Helen Lavery
Janette Loughlin
Radek Maclclak
Megan Magill
Colm McAteer
Aoife McCloskey
Collette McEntee
Sarah McErlain
Patricia McGreevy
Ashlene McGurk
Colin McHugh
Mary McManus
Cathan McRoberts
Catherine Moore
Donal Morgan
Edite Muceniece
Seamus O'Hara
Bernadette Owens
Patrick Quinn
Bobbi Rai Purdy
Geraldine Reynolds
Hayley Russell
Michael Shotton
Ciara Ward
Susannah Wilson

Volunteers
Jordyn Cummings
Bernadette Fox
Jennifer Kerr
Jake Kieran
Alana McAlister
Melissa Patty

LYRIC THEATRE SUPPORTERS

Principal Funder

Also Funded by

Main Stage Sponsor

Corporate Lounge Sponsor

The Lyric Theatre is also generously supported by

In-Kind Sponsors

DIRECT WINE SHIPMENTS

Young Vic
It's a big world in here

The Cut Bar & Restaurant
Our bar and restaurant is a relaxing place to meet and eat. An inspired mix of classic and original play-themed dishes made from fresh, free-range and organic ingredients creates an exciting menu.
www.thecutbar.com

Our shows
We present the widest variety of classics, new plays, forgotten works and music theatre. We tour and co-produce extensively within the UK and internationally.

Our artists
Our shows are created by some of the world's great theatre people alongside the most adventurous of the younger generation. This fusion makes us one of the most exciting theatres in the world.

Our audience
...is famously the youngest and most diverse in London. We encourage those who don't think theatre is 'for them' to make it part of their lives. We give 10 per cent of our tickets to schools and neighbours irrespective of box-office demand, and keep prices low.

Our partners near at hand
Each year we engage with 10,000 local people – individuals and groups of all kinds including schools and colleges – by exploring theatre on and offstage. From time to time we invite our neighbours to appear on our stage alongside professionals.

Our partners further away
By co-producing with leading theatre, opera, and dance companies from London and around the world we create shows neither partner could achieve alone.

The Young Vic is a company limited by guarantee, registered in England No. 1188209.

VAT registration No. 236 673 348

The Young Vic (registered charity number 268876) receives public funding from:

markit
Lead sponsor of the Young Vic's funded ticket scheme

Get more from the Young Vic Online

 youngvictheatre

 @youngvictheatre

 youngviclondon

 youngviclondon.wordpress.com

 @youngvictheatre

Sign up to receive email updates at **youngvic.org/register**

THE YOUNG VIC COMPANY

Artistic Director
David Lan
Executive Director
Lucy Woollatt

Associate Artistic Director
Sue Emmas
Lead Producer
Daisy Heath
Producer
Ben Cooper

Genesis Fellow
Gbolahan Obisesan

ASSOCIATES
Associate Designer
Jeremy Herbert
Associate Artists
Joe Hill-Gibbins
Julia Horan
Ian MacNeil
Sacha Wares
International Associates
Benedict Andrews
Gísli Örn Gardarsson
Amir Nizar Zuabi
Associate Companies
1927
Belarus Free Theatre
BirdGang
Good Chance Theatre
Regional Theatre Young Directors Scheme

ADMINISTRATION
Assistant Producer
Iain Goosey
Administration Manager
Nastasia Tryphonos
Database Administrator
Lee-Anne Inglis
Administrator to the Producers
Tamara Moore

Assistant to the Artistic Director
Andrew Hughes

DEVELOPMENT
Director of Development & Future Partnerships
Livvy Brinson
Development Manager
Reed Nykiforuk

Research Officer
Natasha Ratter
Development Assistant
Vanessa Onwuemezi

FINANCE
Finance Manager
Sophie Wells
Finance and Contracts Assistant
Janine Carter

FRONT OF HOUSE
Theatre Manager
Paul Marshall
Front of House Manager
Will Bowden
Operations Assistant
Frank Osborne
Duty Managers
Liz Arday
Martin Dickinson
Megan Griffith
Claire Harris
Matt Hatt
Ushers
Simone Bell
Clair Burningham
Debbie Burningham
Oliver Byng
Billy Cullum
Laura Day
Francesca De Sica
Eboni Dixon
Sile Edwards
Adrian Gardner
Tom Hadrill
Susan Harrold
Owen Haslegrave
Shermin Hassan
William Heslop
Nicole Jacobs
Toheeb Jimoh
Grace Kayibanda
Aaron Kelly
Lynn Knight
Radi Kopacki
George Mills
Glenn Mortimer
Taz Munyaneza
Sheila Murphy
Tobi Oludipe
Nadine Pacquette
Julie Patten
Mariko Primarolo
Gracjana Rejmer-Canovas
Nathan Rumney
Thea Sandall
Joanna Selcott
Paula Shaw

Jack Sturt
Mark Vanderstoop
Isaac Vincent
Eve Williams
Dan Young

MARKETING AND PRESS
Director of Marketing and Press
Stacy Coyne
Press Manager
Charlotte Bayley
Ticketing Manager
James Orr
Marketing Manager
Julia Evans
Communications Officer
Leon Puplett
Press and Marketing Officer
Beanie Ridler
Press and Publications Assistant
Christine Achampong

PRODUCTION
Technical Director
Igor
Company Manager
Anna Cole
Acting Head of Stage
Hilary Williamson
Head of Lighting
Nicki Brown
Head of Costume
Catherine Kodicek
Production Manager (Studios)
Neil Mickel
Workshop Manager
Emma Hayward
Senior Sound Technician
Amy Bramma
Senior Lighting Technician
Nicole Smith
Senior Costume Technician
Kinnetia Isidore
Stage Technician
Nick Aldrich
Studio Technician
Nell Allen
Production Administrator
Rachel Salenius
Costume Apprentice
Rianna Azoro

TAKING PART
Director of Taking Part
Imogen Brodie
Schools and Colleges Project Manager
Georgia Dale
Participation Project Manager
Rob Lehmann
Two Boroughs & Directors Programme Project Manager
Kirsten Adam
Taking Part and Administration Assistant
Daniel Harrison

WELCOME TEAM
Welcome Team Manager
Ciara O'Toole
Welcome Team
Johanna Keane
Chris Stevens
Josh Husselbee
Maryam Shofowora
Nick Hafezi

BOARD
Patrick McKenna (Chair)
Sean Egan
David Fletcher
Sarah Hall
Rory Kinnear
Carol Lake
David Lan
Anna Lane
Ivan Lewis MP
Rita Skinner
Steve Tompkins
Bill Winters

DEVELOPMENT BOARD
Rita Skinner (Chair)
Rotha Bell
Beatrice Bondy
Caroline Cormack
Annabel Duncan-Smith
Anna Lane
Jill Manson
Will Meldrum
Chris Organ
Barbara Reeves
Mark Selby
Bill Winters

ON LEAVE
Lily Einhorn

SUPPORTING THE YOUNG VIC

The Young Vic relies on the generous support of many individuals, trusts, foundations, and companies to produce our work, on and off stage. For their recent support we thank

Public Funders
Arts Council England
Big Lottery Fund
British Council
Creative & Cultural Skills
Lambeth Borough Council
Southwark Council

Corporate Partners
American Express
Barclays
Berkeley Group
Markit
Wahaca

Corporate Members
aka
Bloomberg
Clifford Chance
Ingenious Media PLC
Memery Crystal
Royal Bank of Scotland
and NatWest

Partners and Upper Circle
Lionel Barber & Victoria
Greenwood
The Bickertons
Tony & Gisela Bloom
Simon & Sally Borrows
Sandra Cavlov
Caroline & Ian Cormack
Manfred & Lydia Gorvy
Patrick Handley
Jack & Linda Keenan
Chris & Jane Lucas
Patrick McKenna
Simon & Midge Palley
Karl-Johan Persson
Barbara Reeves
Jon & NoraLee Sedmak
Dasha Shenkman
Justin Shinebourne
Rita & Paul Skinner
Bruno Wang
Anda & Bill Winters

Soul Mates
David & Corinne Abbott
Jane Attias
Clive Bannister
Chris & Frances Bates
Ginny & Humphrey Battcock
Anthony & Karen Beare
Joanne Beckett
Royce & Rotha Bell
Lady Primrose Bell
Sarah Billinghurst Solomon
Adrian & Lisa Binks
Eva Boenders & Scott Stevens
Beatrice Bondy
Katie Bradford
CJ & LM Braithwaite
Simone Brych-Nourry
Clive & Helena Butler
Lucy & Spencer de Grey
Annabel Duncan-Smith
Sean Egan
Jennifer & Jeff Eldredge
Don Ellwood & Sandra Johnigan

Lysbeth Fox
Paul Gambaccini
Sarah Gay Fletcher
Jill & Jack Gerber
Beth & Gary Glynn
Annika Goodwille
Katherine Hallgarten
Sarah Hall
Richard Hardman & Family
Frances Hellman
Madeleine Hodgkin
Nik Holttum & Helen Brannigan
Jane Horrocks
Linden Ife
Maxine Isaacs
Clive Jones
Tom Keatinge
John Kennedy
John Kinder & Gerry Downey
Mr & Mrs Herbert Kretzmer
Carol Lake
Martha Lane Fox
Patti Laskawy
Jude Law
Victoria Leggett
Chris & Jane Lucas
Tony Mackintosh
James & Sue Macmillan
Jill & Justin Manson
Lady Medina Marks
Michael McCabe
Karen McHugh
Sir Ian McKellen
Juliet Medforth
Barbara Minto
Hala Mnaymneh
Joseph Morgan
Miles Morland
Georgia Oetker
Sally O'Neill
Rob & Lesley O'Rahilly
Julia Palca
Tim & Lynn Payne
André Ptaszynski
Steve Richards
Anthony & Sally Salz
Ron & Sue Sandler
Catherine Schreiber
Charles & Donna Scott
Carol Sellars
Dr. Bhagat Sharma
Jenny Sheridan
Lois Sieff
Nicola Stanhope
Sir Patrick Stewart
Karen Taylor
Jan & Michael Topham
Totally Theatre Productions
The Ulrich Family
Donna & Richard Vinter
Jimmy & Carol Walker
Rob & Gillian Wallace
Edgar & Judith Wallner

Trust Supporters
Amberstone Trust
Andor Charitable Trust
Austin & Hope Pilkington Trust
Backstage Trust

Boris Karloff Charitable
Foundation
Boshier Hinton Foundation
The Burford Cannell Charitable
Trust
The City Bridge Trust
The Cleopatra Trust
Clifford Chance Foundation
Clore Duffield Foundation
Cockayne – Grants for the Arts
John S Cohen Foundation
The Co-operative Membership
Community Fund
David Laing Foundation
The Dr. Mortimer and Theresa
Sackler Foundation
D'Oyly Carte Charitable Trust
Embassy of the Kingdom of the
Netherlands
Equitable Charitable Trust
The Eranda Rothschild
Foundation
Ernest Cook Trust
The Foyle Foundation
Garfield Weston Foundation
Garrick Charitable Trust
Genesis Foundation
Golden Bottle Trust
Golsoncott Foundation
H&M Foundation
The Harold Hyam Wingate
Foundation
Jerwood Charitable Foundation
Joanies Fund
John Thaw Foundation
J. Paul Getty Jnr. Charitable
Trust
The Kidron and Hall Family
The Leche Trust
The Limbourne Trust
The London Community
Foundation
The Mackintosh Foundation
Martin Bowley Charitable Trust
Mrs Margaret Guido's Charitable
Trust
Newcomen Collett Foundation
The Noel Coward Foundation
Paul Hamlyn Foundation
The Portrack Charitable Trust
The Rayne Trust
The Red Hill Trust
Richard Radcliffe Charitable Trust
The Richenthal Foundation
Royal Norwegian Embassy
Royal Victoria Hall Foundation
The Sackler Trust
Unity Theatre Trust
Sir Walter St John's Educational
Charity
The Wolfson Foundation

And with thanks to all the Young
Vic Friends and those donors who
wish to remain anonymous.

markit®

Proud to be the lead sponsor of the Funded Ticket Programme

Through Markit's support, the Young Vic offers nearly 10,000 free tickets to young people and many that would not otherwise be able to enjoy the theatre

THE NEST

Franz Xaver Kroetz

In a new translation by Conor McPherson

Characters

KURT
MARTHA

This text went to press before the end of rehearsals and so may differ slightly from the play as performed.

ACT ONE

Scene One

Late evening in the apartment. On the sofa, KURT *lies asleep in the flickering light of the television. The volume is turned off.* MARTHA *sits at a table with her work in front of her. She holds a receiver to her ear as she speaks on the phone.*

MARTHA. Good evening. May I speak to the head of the household please? Hello, I'm calling on behalf of Incorporated Research Group Limited, conducting research into banking practice and preferences in the...

She is cut off. She makes a note, looks at the next number on her list, dials and checks her watch, making a note.

Good evening. May I speak to the head of the household please? Thank you. (*Waits.*) Hello, I'm calling on behalf of Incorporated Research Group Limited, conducting market research into banking practice and preferences in your area, with whom am I speaking please? Yes, it's one minute to nine o'clock. (*Pause.*) We call up till nine o'clock. Is there a time that would be more convenient? The questionnaire takes seven minutes. I see. Well I'm sorry for any inconvenience. Thank you, too.

She hangs up. She sits looking at the table disconsolately for a moment. KURT *talks to someone in his sleep. She looks over at him. She gets up. She is visibly pregnant. Her back is sore. She leans on a chair, stretching to get some relief. She goes over to the couch and looks down at* KURT, *willing him to wake up. She picks up the TV remote control and presses the volume button. A voice suddenly explodes from the TV: 'As a further ten thousand strikers descended upon the factory the police were ordered to make their first baton charge.'* KURT *sits up, wondering where he is.* MARTHA *laughs and switches the TV off.*

KURT. I was watching that!

MARTHA. You've been asleep for half an hour!

KURT. What happened to the guy in the end?

MARTHA. I don't know. I was working.

KURT. Well, I'll tell you. That was, without question, the worst depiction of a lorry driver yet seen on TV – and that's saying something!

MARTHA *is tidying away their dinner plates*.

MARTHA. Well in fairness he was hardly driving a lorry, Kurt. He had a little van.

KURT. Well, this is it – it's a whole other story once you get a HGV licence. I mean it's a whole other world. Nobody realises.

MARTHA. He looked a bit like you though, didn't he?

KURT. What?!

MARTHA. Except for his ears.

KURT. His ears were a bleeding joke, man! Jaysus, what a clown! If my wife told me she wasn't gonna have my baby I'd tell her, 'Yes you bleeding well are!'

MARTHA. Charming!

KURT. He was afraid of his own fucking baby! (*Rubs his face*.) God, I keep falling asleep.

MARTHA. Get into bed.

KURT. Yeah. You finished here?

MARTHA. Yeah.

KURT *starts to convert their sofa into a bed*. MARTHA *stands leaning against the sink, staring into space*.

KURT. If that moron did half the overtime I do… What happened to him in the end? (*Pause*.) Are you alright?

MARTHA. What? (*Short pause*.) Yeah.

KURT. How many did you do?

MARTHA. Uh! One old woman took the questionnaire, and then told me she had no bank account! Then three 'no thank you's and it was nine o'clock.

KURT. What a waste. How many is that today?

MARTHA. Thirty-eight.

KURT. That's not bad, though.

MARTHA. Your woman, Nina, the supervisor says the average is a hundred a day.

KURT (*as though this is a reasonable target*). Ten an hour.

MARTHA. Yeah.

KURT. Listen – forty euros is not nothing.

MARTHA. The booklet says people can make up to two hundred.

KURT. You're not even supposed to be working!

MARTHA. It's just talking on the phone.

KURT. You'll get there. You'll be breaking their records in a few weeks.

MARTHA. I don't know. (*Notices that* KURT *is far away.*) What?

KURT. What? Oh no – just listening. You hear that siren? In the distance?

MARTHA *listens. It's barely audible.*

MARTHA (*affirmative*). Mm-hm.

KURT *resumes fixing their bed up.*

KURT. I always love it when you hear a siren pass by. You always think, 'It's not me. Whoever it is they're after – it wasn't me – 'cause I didn't do it.' And you just think, you know – (*Clenches his fist in triumph.*) 'Yes!'

MARTHA (*humouring him, without quite getting on board*).
Your conscience is clear, Kurt.

KURT (*points at her as though she has said something very wise
he wishes he'd thought of*). Now. (*A little pause, he resumes
making the bed*.) Fucking motorbike cop knocks on the door
of my cab today, says 'What do you think you're playing at?'
'I'm resting,' I say. 'This is not a layby,' he goes, 'it's the hard
shoulder.' 'Alright!' I say, 'Keep your bleeding hair on!'
'What's in the back?' he goes. 'Four and a half thousand
gallons of milk,' I tell him. 'Where are you going with it?'
he says. 'To the bleeding dairy! Where do you think I'm
bleeding going with it?' I say. I can tell by his stupid face he
doesn't have a clue how to climb up and check the container.
I just stare him out of it. 'Alright,' he goes, 'Move it.' And
I just thought, 'What a wanker. What was all that about?'

MARTHA *has joined him at the bed. Her only reaction to
his story is a tiny snort.* KURT *regards her.*

Are you still happy with me?

MARTHA. Why wouldn't I be? You're behaving yourself,
aren't you?

KURT. Yeah, no, I am. I just. There was a time when you…
thought I was a bit of a…

MARTHA. Oh don't start banging on about all that again!

KURT. Listen, only 'cause it's true! (*As though this still rankles*.)
There was a time you wanted nothing to do with me!

MARTHA. When you're young you don't know your arse from
your elbow. You have to be allowed to make mistakes. That's
the way I look at it now.

KURT. Am I a mistake?

MARTHA. No. You're not a mistake. And even if you are
you're a lucky one.

She strokes his hair.

He's moving. Do you want a listen?

KURT *nods and puts his ear to her tummy. Pause.*

KURT. I can't hear anything.

MARTHA. Whenever you listen he always stops straight away.

KURT. He knows it's his dad.

MARTHA. He must!

Pause.

KURT. I still... you know...

MARTHA. Well you'll just have to control yourself.

KURT. I read in the paper you can do it right up until the day of the birth.

MARTHA. What paper?

KURT. *The Daily Star.*

MARTHA. Well I'd rather do what the doctor says and not *The Daily Star*, alright? Three months before, and three months after.

KURT. That's six months!

MARTHA. And?

Pause.

KURT. I'm just saying.

MARTHA. Just go asleep instead.

KURT. Yeah, that's...

They lie there for a minute. KURT *gets up.*

MARTHA. Where are you going?

KURT. Where do you think?

MARTHA. Come here, I'll do it.

KURT. No, I'll be quicker.

He goes.

Scene Two

The flat. Saturday afternoon. MARTHA *is at the table with her baby-shopping lists, laptop, etc.* KURT *comes from the bathroom.*

KURT. Okay – here we go.

MARTHA. Now it's going to be shocking at first okay?

KURT. I'm not going be shocked, believe me.

MARTHA. I've researched everything to the last penny.

KURT. Okay, just hit me.

MARTHA. And Edel was helping me with it.

KURT. I'm sure she was!

MARTHA. She has three kids, Kurt!

KURT. That's what I'm saying.

MARTHA. She gave me two hours of her own time.

KURT. She's a good friend.

MARTHA (*sick of his sarcasm*). Ugh! Okay, buggy. Buggy's the hardest one because there's so much to decide. I wish you'd have come with me.

KURT. Why?

MARTHA. Because the new models all have new features and it all gets so confusing.

KURT. Just get the newest model!

MARTHA. They come with or without all the features though.

KURT. Like what?

MARTHA. Like a little window in the hood so you can see the baby and it's not so dark.

KURT. Get the window.

MARTHA. It's two hundred and eighty-six euro, though. The one without it is two hundred and thirty.

KURT (*raises his hand and speaks like an authority, or a judge*).
Approved! Next!

MARTHA. We're still on the buggy. You can get a fitted
mattress as well, it's only thirty euros. Everybody gets it.

KURT. The child has to sleep. Approved! Next!

MARTHA. We're going to be saving a lot because Edel is
gonna lend us her cot and her baby scales.

KURT (*with disgust*). We don't want to be borrowing other
people's beds!

MARTHA. Kurt, it's what everybody does, you only need a cot
for the first year. We'll give it back and Edel will give it to
her sister. Nobody buys one.

KURT. Alright, approved. Next!

MARTHA. Okay. Two small Liegelind under-mattresses –
they're only nineteen euros each. (*Crosses something off the
list.*) I already have some shorts and tops. And then he'll
need a big Liegeland under-mattress.

KURT. But you just said we're already getting two small ones!

MARTHA. But he'll need a big one.

KURT. Why?

MARTHA. Let's just keep doing the sums and we can come
back, okay?

KURT. Go on.

MARTHA. McKinnon baby sleeping bag, fifty-one euros,
four sets of sheets for the cot – twenty euros each – that's all
a hundred and thirty-one. Laura Lee baby soap dish, three
twenty-five, Laura Lee baby hairbrush – and comb – ten
twenty-five. Soames Bros. milk thermometer, eight eighty,
Rag and Bone fold-up nappy-changing mat twenty-three
forty, Rafael baby bath thirty-two euro, stand for baby bath
to sit in the big bath, thirty-two fifty, McKinnon baby bottle
holder, seven fifty and – oh yeah – this is a question for you:

Do we buy an electric bottle warmer? Forty-one euros, saves loads of time apparently – especially in the middle of the night and you're not washing so many pots all the time.

KURT. But you have time. You're not working.

MARTHA. I'm working from home.

KURT. Is it normal? For people to get one?

MARTHA. If they can afford it.

KURT (*raises his hand*). Approved! Next!

MARTHA. No you're right! It is better! Six Advent wide-necked bottles – you get them all together it's only eighteen euros – and a steriliser unit, so… no hold on – (*Making a note.*) That's the pharmacy section! What's that doing there? (*Laughs.*)

KURT (*not sharing the laugh*). Good one!

MARTHA. Oh no!

KURT. What.

MARTHA. This is all the old list! What am I doing ? I did a new list last night!

She gets up and starts rummaging around.

What did you do with my orange folder?

KURT. I have no idea what you're talking about.

MARTHA. This is pointless now!

KURT. Oh God! Just keep going with this list, will ya? It'll give us an idea! And if there's any changes…

MARTHA. They say this happens to your brain.

KURT. This happened to your brain a long time ago.

MARTHA. Well thanks very much.

KURT. The brain event.

MARTHA. Look I'll just keep going. Now, Kurt, this is kind of for me, but we'll really need a maternity bra, probably two. And I'm just going to need new clothes. Like I just will…

KURT. Of course! Approved! (*Like he can't believe she would even consider that he'd deny her this*.) Jaysus!

MARTHA. Now – tricky one... Edel will let us have her cot quilt and a mattress and baby blanket, but they're all second-hand.

KURT. My baby doesn't need anything second-hand.

MARTHA. They're actually nice things...

KURT. No!

MARTHA. Good, I agree. Quilt is about seventy euros, the mattress is forty-four, baby blanket, depends, but let's say forty. Now here's another one for you. Edel told me about this new aloe vera vitamin-E oil. It's supposed to be brilliant for stretch marks.

KURT. Stretch marks?

MARTHA. Yeah. This oil is supposed to be brilliant but it's dear.

KURT. How much?

MARTHA. Thirty euros a bottle, but it lasts about ten days. I should have been using it already apparently.

KURT. Well start on it then. I don't want a load of stretch marks all over the shop and you know what as well? If you go easy? You'll probably get two weeks out of a bottle.

MARTHA. Great, I'll get it. You know I want to be gorgeous again after the baby.

KURT. You're gorgeous now.

MARTHA *smiles*.

You're my everything. You know that. But stretch marks – that's not gonna be good.

MARTHA. Don't worry, it says online that giving birth is like a total spa rejuvenation for the body – especially when it's a boy.

KURT. Then how lucky are we?

MARTHA. Okay, so let's keep going. Now look, you don't have to have a baby-changer unit, I can change him on the floor or the bed, but that wrecks your back apparently.

KURT. Then get one.

MARTHA. The one I have my eye on isn't cheap.

KURT. No shit. Remember the day we were getting my new suit and your man goes, 'Your wife has an eye for the finer things.'

MARTHA. What's wrong with that?

KURT. I didn't say there was anything wrong with it. Just, you know…

MARTHA. Just what?

KURT. Just nothing! Approved! Next!

MARTHA. Okay. Nappies and wipes.

KURT. Well we're not gonna not have nappies!

MARTHA. I know, but just for the budget. (*Scribbling on the list.*) I'm putting in a hundred and fifty for stuff from the chemist and that book the doctor told us to get, and there's another one I want to get off Amazon called *The Child in the Woman's Body*.

KURT. Listen, it's good to know the story.

MARTHA. That's what the doctor said. Okay so – that's it. For now. Unless you have anything.

KURT. Yeah – I do. Seventy-five euro for a new digital camera.

MARTHA. God! I'd have forgotten about that!

KURT. Not me. You want to capture the whole moment. Oh and fifty euros, 'cause I want to get his name tattooed on my leg when he's born.

MARTHA. What?!

KURT. Mick Morris in the warehouse has all his kids right down both his calf muscles with the dates and the times they were born, all done in this kind of *Lord of the Rings* kind of writing. It's why he always wears shorts.

MARTHA. Kurt, if you even think of doing that.

KURT. I'm only messing! He's a fucking idiot!

MARTHA. You better be. Okay. Do you want to do it? (*Add it all up*.)

KURT. Leave it to beaver.

She gives him the list and he starts to add it all up on his phone. MARTHA *goes to get a drink.*

Everything... is... approved. We should get a little stamper so I can stamp everything when I approve it.

MARTHA. You probably do want one!

KURT. It'd be good wouldn't it? 'Approved! Next!' 'Hey! Here, this is not approved! Where's the stamp? Where is it?!'

MARTHA. I'll stamp you.

KURT. Two thousand and twenty-six euros and thirty cents exactly.

MARTHA. God I thought it was gonna be up around three thousand.

KURT. Listen. It probably will be by the time we put on all the things we've forgotten. I told Ray Charles in work, 'A kid costs you ten grand, man, no matter what way you wanna look at it.'

MARTHA. Yeah, like once he's here. It's just gonna be more and more.

KURT. I'll bring in the dosh. And you don't worry about it. (*Points at the list*.) Approved.

Scene Three

The allotment. MARTHA *is kneeling, weeding some pots.*
KURT *wheels on a barrow of compost and starts putting it in a hole.*

KURT. The frost killed all those little daffs over there.

MARTHA. I know. It's sad really.

KURT. Ah we'll grow more.

    MARTHA *gets up.*

MARTHA. You don't mind how tired I get, Kurt?

KURT. Of course not!

MARTHA. I just have no energy today.

KURT. Don't be ridiculous. You're supposed to be taking it easy, go and sit down.

MARTHA. Just for a few minutes. You don't mind?

KURT. Sit there for the whole afternoon!

    MARTHA *goes and sits down. She watches* KURT *working.*

MARTHA. You're so good with nature.

KURT. I always was. You remember what my dad said? 'We're too old for the allotment now, but it'll be in good hands.'

MARTHA. He was right.

KURT. It's in better shape now than they ever had it. (*Looks up at the sky.*) You hear me, you old bugger?

    They both smile. MARTHA *watches* KURT *working.*

MARTHA. You know what I'm thinking about?

KURT. The baby?

MARTHA. Bingo.

KURT. How did I know that?

MARTHA. I was just thinking that one day he'll be running around in here. And we'll be watching him and thinking about how happy we are.

KURT. Yeah, well I've been thinking about it too. And I'll tell you one thing – there'll be no messing about. He can't be getting in the beds, we'll tell him where he can walk and he better behave because otherwise – (*Whistles and indicates with his thumb 'get lost'.*)

MARTHA. Ah he'll only be a baby! What can he do?

KURT. Start as you mean to go on! That's my motto. But I have a plan. Do you know what I'm gonna do? You see over there? Sandpit.

MARTHA. Oh he'll love a sandpit!

KURT. But no sand over here. It'll wreck the soil. So let him stay over there and you won't have to be giving out to him all the time.

MARTHA. I won't be giving out to him! Only if he's bold.

KURT. And I'm gonna build a fence around it.

MARTHA. Ah Kurt! Just let him learn. How is he supposed to figure things out for himself if we don't teach him?

MARTHA *watches* KURT *working*.

KURT. Not everybody has a nice allotment. You have to appreciate it.

MARTHA. That's what I'm saying though.

MARTHA *watches* KURT *work*.

Scene Four

It's night-time at the flat. KURT *is eating his dinner. He is silent. He seems removed.* MARTHA *sits with a cup of herbal tea. They are silent for few moments.* KURT *idly glances through a magazine.*

MARTHA. You know the ad where the woman says she has a bad conscience?

KURT. What? Oh yeah.

MARTHA. I have a bad conscience.

KURT. Why?

MARTHA. Same reason she does.

KURT. Why does she have a bad conscience?

MARTHA. Do you feel itchy?

KURT. No.

MARTHA. I stopped buying Lenor.

KURT. Buying what?

MARTHA. Fabric softener.

KURT. Why?

MARTHA. You said to try and cut back on the…

KURT. I didn't mean washing powder! Jaysus! I told you I'm bringing in the money!

MARTHA. Kurt, be nice to me tonight, I'm all over the place.

KURT. What?

MARTHA *brings a tissue to her face and closes her eyes, silently crying.*

I told you I'd talk to the boss! I have first dibs on overtime. So don't be fucking about with the washing… up liquid for Jaysus' sake! Come on, Martha, it's alright. He's a decent skin. I never really spoke to him before but he's…

MARTHA. He knows we need it.

KURT. He has two kids himself. He said, 'Listen you don't
need to tell me about it, Kurt. I'll look after you,' he says.
'Extra haulage, it's all yours.' Poor fucker is always under
the kosh from the union. Their new one is they won't allow
anyone drive more than fifty-six hours a week because of
their mental health. I fucking said it to them, 'There's more
to life than mental health you know! It's not the be-all and
end-all!'

MARTHA. I'm sorry.

KURT. Don't be sorry. (*Points to her tummy.*) That little fella is
wrecking your bleeding head already!

She laughs.

Look at this. When we're in the clear and I can put the
overtime away – for us – check it out. Eight cylinder front-
mounted engine, five thousand three hundred and fifty cc,
three hundred brake-horsepower, overhead valves, fourway
downdraft carburetor, fully synchronised four-speed
transmission – or optional manual gearbox, individual front
suspension, De Dion rear axle with hydraulic suspension self-
locking differential, top speed two hundred and forty kmh!

MARTHA. What is it? A car?

KURT. Yeah, it's a car. Of course it's a car! What do you think
it is?

MARTHA. Well I thought it might be a lorry, I don't know!
How much is that?

KURT. You could get one second-hand, third-hand… fifty grand?

MARTHA. I meant the magazine.

KURT. This?

MARTHA. Is that the price? Ten fifty?

KURT. No – that's the English price.

MARTHA. So it's more than that?

KURT. Are you gonna deny me once or twice a year I might buy this? It's only to have a look at – I mean one day – in the future.

MARTHA. It'll be far in the future.

KURT. Well I think it's good to have a… have a bit of a…

MARTHA. I went into town this morning. Spoke to your woman, Nina. About getting some hours back again when the baby's older.

KURT. Would you stop, Martha!

MARTHA. I thought I better square it all off, so she'd understand.

KURT. Who cares what she understands?

MARTHA. She left me waiting in the corridor! Then out she comes with her coat on. Said they hadn't the space on the roster. Said she'd keep me on file but it was 'highly unlikely' they'd need me back. And she just left. So I just picked up my stuff and when I was going out, you know what had happened? I found her at the bottom of the stairwell – she'd fallen down the stairs.

KURT. Where?

MARTHA. In their building. There was no one else there. She had blood going down her leg. Her tights were all torn. All I had was a few tissues. She didn't even thank me.

KURT. She was too embarrassed.

MARTHA. And you know what? I couldn't even hate her any more.

KURT (*shrugs as though it's self-evident*). That's what God gives you. You're better off out of there. You need to take care of number one now. And number two.

MARTHA. I just want to get through the next three weeks. That's if he's on time.

KURT (*as though she is casting aspersions on his son*). He'll be on time.

Scene Five

MARTHA *sits in a shaft of sunlight in a chair at the hospital.*
She holds her baby in her arms. KURT *comes in with a bunch*
of flowers.

Long pause. MARTHA *beams.*

MARTHA (*very quietly*). There he is.

  KURT *nods.*

  Your son.

  Pause.

  Do you see him?

  KURT *nods. Pause.*

  Do you like him?

  KURT *nods.* MARTHA *laughs.*

KURT. Yes.

  KURT *smiles and nods and looks. He starts to cry.*

  Yes.

ACT TWO

Scene One

KURT *sits holding the baby in a little bundle on his knee.*

KURT (*in a soft voice as though the baby is falling asleep*). Yes,
 you do. Yes, you do. I know. Yes. You're very tired. Oh yes.
 Oh yes. You go, you fall asleep. You go. I'm here. I'm here.
 (*Sings softly.*) The bells of the angelus are calling to say, bong
 bong bong bong bong bong bong bong bing bong. Bong bong
 bong… (*The baby is asleep. Whispers.*) I love you.

MARTHA. What about me?

KURT. You too.

Scene Two

A beautiful lakeside under the trees. MARTHA *and* KURT
wheel their bicycles to the shore and take it all in. MARTHA
has the baby in a papoose on her chest.

MARTHA. Wow.

KURT. Ha?

MARTHA. It's beautiful.

KURT. You see? Stick with me.

MARTHA. I will.

> *They start to spread a blanket and get a picnic out.*
> MARTHA *glances at* KURT. *She takes her T-shirt off to*
> *reveal a demure two-piece swimsuit.*

KURT *sees her.*

KURT. That's nice!

MARTHA. Do you like it? It was only twelve euros in Penneys.

KURT. Twelve euros! You're like something out of a documentary about the South of France or somewhere.

MARTHA. Do you like it?

KURT. It's beautiful.

KURT starts picking food out of a box, munching.

I'm gonna build him a big castle with a moat all around it.

MARTHA. He's too young.

KURT. He'll still learn. This is when their minds are taking it all in.

MARTHA. Kurt. What do you see?

KURT. Where?

MARTHA. When you look at me.

KURT. I see… I see you, you know?

MARTHA. I've changed so much though.

KURT. No you haven't!

MARTHA. You must be blind then!

KURT. It's so gradual you don't notice.

MARTHA (*not what she was looking for*). Thanks.

KURT. Come here.

He holds her.

You're even sexier now, you know that?

MARTHA. Really?

KURT. I'm serious.

He starts growling while he nuzzles her neck. She laughs.

There's something about you making a baby inside you. It drives me crazy.

MARTHA. Kurt! Stefan will see!

KURT. He hasn't a clue.

MARTHA. You just said he's taking it all in.

She gets away from him.

KURT. Well, I'll tell you, I'm taking it all in.

MARTHA *laughs. She looks out across the water.* KURT *eats some grub.*

MARTHA. It's so beautiful here.

KURT. I don't think there's an inch of this country I don't know by now.

MARTHA. God knows you've driven all over it.

KURT. And back. Is he gone back asleep?

MARTHA. The country air has knocked him out.

KURT. I mean, I'd prefer to work, even on a day like this.

MARTHA. Oh stop banging on, will you? One day off in six months and you haven't shut up about it.

KURT. Listen, someone has to keep the show on the road. That little bollocks is expensive, you know.

MARTHA. Don't call him that.

KURT. I'm only joking.

MARTHA. Don't joke like that.

KURT *sighs.*

KURT. Do you think he'd like a swim?

MARTHA. You'll wake him up.

KURT. No, I mean when he's awake.

MARTHA. Maybe after I've fed him. A little paddle.

KURT. Well I'm not gonna fuck him in the water, am I?

MARTHA. Kurt. Do you have to use that kind of language?

KURT. He's asleep.

MARTHA. He still hears it.

They sit looking at the lake.

KURT. Look at the water.

MARTHA. Mmm. I know.

KURT. Still, it'd be great if there was a little bit more work.

MARTHA. Kurt. Can you not just enjoy the day?

KURT. No, I can. I'm just thinking.

Scene Three

KURT *and* MARTHA *are asleep in the apartment under their duvet. The cot stands nearby.* KURT *is talking in his sleep.* MARTHA *wakes up. She switches on the light and looks at* KURT. KURT *whimpers like a child.*

KURT. No, no. No…

MARTHA. Kurt? Kurty?

She shakes him. KURT *wakes with a start.*

KURT. Yeah?

MARTHA. You're having a bad dream.

KURT. Why?

MARTHA. I don't know.

Pause.

KURT. I was in my lorry. The load was slipping down over us.

MARTHA. Was I there?

KURT. We were all there. (*Bursts out laughing with a kind of relief.*) What am I like?

MARTHA *can't help laughing.*

The load could ever come down over the cab! Did I wake you?

MARTHA. I was awake.

KURT. Why were you awake?

MARTHA. I don't know.

KURT. Rip Van Winkle is still asleep.

MARTHA. Until he wants his bottle.

KURT. You know what it is? You always put too much mayonnaise in the turkey.

MARTHA. No I don't.

KURT. We can't digest it!

MARTHA. You never take a break. That's more like what it is. Any chance of a few euros and you're gone.

KURT. No I'm not! Do you want for anything?

MARTHA. Just my husband.

KURT. You want me in here under your feet more?

MARTHA. I don't think you know how hard it is with a baby, Kurt.

KURT. You need to go out more.

MARTHA. It's just too hard with him, though.

KURT. You don't try. (*Pause.*) Three thousand four hundred and fifty euros this month after tax. You know how many people get that in this economy? The way it is now? Not many.

MARTHA. I could work. You could mind Stefan a bit more.

KURT. Have you lost your mind? The immigrant workers, all the kebab-heads loading the lorries are getting the axe every

week. It'll be us next. I'm not telling the boss I want to go
home and mind the baby! He'll tell me to bleeding stay there!

MARTHA. He likes you, he wouldn't let you go.

KURT. He likes anyone who's not in the union, that's all it is.

MARTHA. He likes you, Kurt.

Pause.

KURT. He has a new run for me.

MARTHA. Really?

KURT. Yeah. On my own.

MARTHA. Well there you go.

KURT. Yeah. Can't tell anyone. Otherwise they'll all be…

MARTHA. Right. God, Kurt, you're sweating.

KURT. No, I'm just hot.

MARTHA. Get a drink.

KURT. Yeah…

Her phone bleeps.

Who's that?

MARTHA *looks.*

MARTHA. My dad.

KURT. Why is he texting in the middle of the night?

MARTHA. 'Cause I'm not talking to him. We were supposed to
meet for a cup of coffee in the park this morning. He fucking
left me sitting there for three quarters of an hour. Never even
called me. Stefan's nose wouldn't stop running, I had to go!
Then on the bus – I see him walking down the street, looking
in the bookies' shop windows like he hasn't a care in the
world, you know what I mean?

KURT. Did you not get off and tell him?

MARTHA. The bus was halfway round the corner. I had Stefan.

KURT. Did you not call him and tell him?

MARTHA. I couldn't be bothered. (*Shrugs*.) I'm finished
    with him.

> KURT *drinks his water*. MARTHA *sits on the bed and looks*
> *at him*.

You know, it's alright now.

KURT. What is?

MARTHA. If you want to.

KURT. What.

MARTHA. If you want to…

KURT. Oh. Oh good. Great.

> *Pause*.

MARTHA. Do you want to?

KURT. Yeah, of course I do. I'm…

MARTHA. If you're too tired…

KURT. No, I'm just, I'm a bit…

MARTHA. I know.

KURT. I'm a bit hot.

MARTHA. Yeah.

KURT. But that's great.

MARTHA. Yeah!

> *She lies down, turning away from* KURT. *He stays where*
> *he is*.

KURT. That's great.

Scene Four

The concealed clearing by the lake. We hear a lorry approach. The engine switches off. KURT *enters carrying the end of a long thick hose pipe. He puts one end in the lake and goes off. We hear the pump start up.* KURT *comes back and stands there texting on his phone while the truck pumps its effluent into the lake. After a while, he stops texting and goes off. The pump stops. The hose is pulled offstage. We hear his lorry start up and drive away.*

Scene Five

The light changes, bringing us to a little while later. MARTHA *wheels her bike to the water's edge. She has the baby in her papoose. She takes out her phone and dials.*

MARTHA. Hi. It's me. You're probably driving. You're not gonna guess where I am. It was so hot in the apartment. Rip Van Winkle fell asleep so I strapped him on and we cycled up to the lake – believe it or not! I'll be home by five, so call me. See you.

She hangs up.

Now, little man. What would Daddy say now? Hm? Up here all by ourselves? Are you smiling at me? Are you smiling? I think you are. Yes, I think you are. Would you like a paddle? I think you would. Would you like a little splish-splash? Will Mommy put you in the water? I think we will. Yes! I think we will. Just let me get your clothes off. Now. We'll be nice and cool in a minute.

She takes Stefan's pants off and puts him in the water. He starts crying.

Don't be silly. It's nice! Is it cold? Is it nice? Don't be silly. Don't be afraid. It's nice! It's nice!

Scene Six

KURT *stands anxiously in a hospital waiting room.* MARTHA *comes in with bandages round her hands.*

MARTHA. You can go in and see him now.

KURT. What did they say?

MARTHA. They won't know how bad the burns are until the other doctor sees them tomorrow. They said I'm not as bad because I'm an adult. They think there was something in the water.

Pause.

KURT. Why did you go there – without me with you?

MARTHA. What?

KURT. You can't be going around these places on your own, without me there.

MARTHA. What could you have done?

KURT. I'd have… I'd have known it wasn't a good idea.

MARTHA. How could you know?

Pause.

KURT. Because it was me.

Long pause.

Scene Seven

They are in their apartment. MARTHA *stands near the cooker. An intense silence.*

KURT. I don't even know if... I'm a... person.

MARTHA. Oh just... shut up!

KURT. I'd swap places with him. I'd do it in a second. (*A grim smile at his helplessness.*) But you just can't! You just...

MARTHA. How can you laugh?

KURT. I'm not laughing – I'm just...

MARTHA. You are – you were!

KURT. No! I wasn't.

Long pause.

MARTHA. I told you to be quiet.

KURT. Yeah. I am. (*Pause.*) We're finished now, aren't we?

MARTHA. Yeah.

KURT. Yeah. I don't blame you. (*Pause.*) No one could live with a man who's killed their child.

MARTHA. That's right.

KURT. But... listen. If he makes it...

MARTHA. What.

Long pause.

KURT. Martha.

MARTHA. What.

KURT. Did you make something to eat?

MARTHA. Excuse me?

KURT. No just did you make something to eat earlier, before... you went up to the lake?

MARTHA. Not for you, no.

KURT. Do you mind if I get something? I'll sit somewhere else.

MARTHA. I can't even sit down.

KURT. I'll just stay over here.

> KURT *goes and starts preparing a sandwich. He suddenly gives voice to his feelings in an outburst, angrily launching at* MARTHA, *startling her.*

> He said it was wine that was gone off!! 'It's not even dangerous! The fish will get a bit tipsy,' he said, he was laughing about it! (*Shouts.*) 'It's just the law – that's all! There's nothing really wrong with it!' he said. 'Just stick it where nobody will see – it's not a big deal!' (*Thumps his chest.*) And I thought I was picked out especially 'cause I have a good brain and he could trust me!! 'Look, there's two hundred euro,' he said, 'that's for you!'

> *He fishes money out of his shirt pocket and shoves it in* MARTHA*'s face. She explodes back at him.*

MARTHA. And if the boss said, 'Hey Kurt, will you chop off your baby's foot for me – it won't kill him – I'll give you two hundred euros!' You'd do that too, wouldn't you? Because the boss told you! The boss, the boss, the boss, the boss, the boss! You're not a man – I don't know how I missed it! – you're a fucking monkey! And the joke is – even the boss is better than you because at least he has half a fucking brain and got a monkey to do his dirty work. And what's worse is I'm married to you. I'm shackled to a trained ape!

KURT. I'm sorry! I'm sorry!

> KURT *tries to hold her. She pushes him away.*

MARTHA (*disgusted*). Get off me! I'm going to the hospital.

KURT. I'll come with you!

MARTHA. You can do what you like, but you're not coming with me.

KURT. I know. It makes your stomach turn doesn't it? When you look at me. I know.

MARTHA. Yes. Yes it does!

KURT. I feel the same! Martha.

She goes. KURT *is alone. Long pause.*

Scene Eight

Early evening in the clearing. The bathing things are still there, just as MARTHA *left them.* KURT *arrives on his bike with a big bag on his back. He goes to the bathing things. Puts his bike down.*

KURT *looks round, embarrassed, uncertain. Then he picks up all the things that* MARTHA *left. He rolls them very carefully together.*

He puts it all on the carrier of his bike and takes a big piece of cardboard from his bag with large letters scrawled on it 'Danger. No Swimming. Poisin' (sic). He takes a broom handle that he has attached to his crossbar and attaches the sign to the broom handle. He shoves the broom handle into the earth.

He picks up his bike again and gets on it.

He stays on the bike by the water's edge. Looks into the water.

Long pause.

He puts the bike down, strips down to his pants. Then he goes very slowly to the water, and walks in.

Pause.

KURT *looks. Then he dips himself in, up to the neck first, and then his head too, so that there is nothing to be seen of him.*

*He stays under for a long time. Then he stands up again, waits,
and goes back to the bank.*

Pause.

*He looks down at himself. Tries to discern any changes.
But there's nothing. While he's doing this he starts shivering.
He waits, tests his skin, nothing.*

ACT THREE

Scene One

Darkness. The apartment. The lights go on. KURT *enters.
His face and hands are red. The skin round his eyes is very red.
He stops. Looks round.*

Pause.

He starts suddenly, for no reason.

Long pause.

*He fetches an old-fashioned clothes line. He sits at the table
and begins to unwind it. He goes to the dresser, takes out some
scissors, cuts off a length of cord. He checks it, pulls it tight.
Measures out another section of the same length. Cuts that off.
He ties them together at both ends, so they're doubled. He puts
them on the table.*

*He looks round. He doesn't know what to do next. He goes
through the whole flat looking for something solid to hang the
rope on. Finds nothing. He goes to the kitchen window, wraps
the rope round the curtain rail and pulls, testing it. This pulls
down the curtain rail and the curtains. He realises that he can
now be seen from outside. He waves across to another window,
acknowledging a neighbour.*

Pause.

*He goes to the bathroom, gets various pills, puts them all on the
table. There's nothing there that might kill him. He is sweating.
He takes a towel and wipes his face.*

Pause.

*He goes into the bathroom, takes out his shaving kit, carries it
to the kitchen table. He sits down. He breaks a plastic
disposable razor. He tries to hold the tiny blade, tries to tape it*

*to something, then decides a knife might be better. He selects
a sharp knife and holds it to his throat. Then he worries about
blood. He stands at the sink with the knife to his throat. He
again realises he can be seen and acknowledges his neighbour.*

He turns out all the lights in the flat.

Pause.

*After a while he turns the lights on again. He is pretty exhausted.
He throws the knife in the sink and starts putting the pills back.*

*He takes his shaving things, is about to take them back to the
bathroom. The front door opens.* MARTHA *comes in. She
stands looking at him. He stands looking down at the table.*

Pause.

MARTHA. He's going to be alright. (*Pause.*) Kurt. Did you
hear me?

KURT *nods.*

What are you doing?

KURT. I was in the water.

MARTHA. What's all this for?

KURT. I was gonna have a shave.

Pause.

MARTHA. He might be able to come home next week. (*Long
pause.*) A good man wouldn't want to kill himself.

KURT. I'm not a good man.

MARTHA. They dropped you in it. The boss lied to you.

KURT (*shrugs*). He knows I'm a stupid person.

Pause.

MARTHA. Look around at everything you've made possible.
All you do is work. All you think about is work, and how to
get more work, and how to make things nice for us. (*Pause.*)
Stefan needs a dad. No matter what you think, don't take
away his father away, Kurt.

KURT. Yeah, well, I couldn't do it anyway. I've been dicking round here for an hour. An ape doesn't know how to kill itself.

MARTHA. I was angry when I said that.

KURT. It's true though.

MARTHA. Kurt, most people are just like you and me. Just doing their best. They don't mean any harm. You didn't know what you were doing – it was an accident.

KURT (*raises his voice*). It wasn't an accident! I always thought I was different to everybody else. But now I know. Someone like me? You can just send me off to do something in the morning, like a little boy going off to the shops. How far will I go before I say no? What can you order me to do before I won't do it? That's not an accident. That's who I am.

MARTHA (*quietly*). I know you better than that, Kurt. You're worn out. We all need to rest now. (*Pause.*) And then, I know you – you'll be out there trying to get the latest bike for Stefan, his own iPad so he can watch his programmes, you'll want to get us a Samsung washing machine. I know you!

Pause.

KURT. No. In the morning… I'm gonna go to the police.

MARTHA. You're gonna report the boss?

KURT. I'm gonna report us both. Him and me.

MARTHA *looks at him as he tidies up his suicide things.*

MARTHA. Kurt, it was a mistake. You won't do anything like that again.

KURT (*shakes his head*). I need everything to be all square – between us.

MARTHA. But they'll take you away!

KURT. Is that what you want me to be!? Some numbskull walking in and out of here that just does what he's told? Is that what you want to be married to?

MARTHA. No! But…

KURT. I can't do that!

MARTHA. But you can't just think of yourself! What about Stefan?!

KURT. I'm thinking about Stefan! What will I say when he's asking me about all the scars on his body and all I can tell him is that it was an 'accident'? 'And I'll tell you another thing, Stefan – I won't be doing any more of *those* jobs for the boss – let him get some other prat to do them!' I can't live like that!

MARTHA. Kurt, you know I want to help you. I do! But you have to help me too and you have to help Stefan. The minute you report the boss you're gonna get the sack, and no one else is going to hire you when they find out what you did!

KURT. Then we'll move away. We'll just have to go somewhere else.

MARTHA. Where!

KURT. Somewhere else! Where nobody knows us. We are who we are and we'll just have to get on with it.

MARTHA. Aw, Kurt, listen to yourself!

KURT. No, Martha, you listen. If we don't do anything about it, it'll just be someone else doing it next month and someone else the month after that. And I'll know they're doing it! It'll always be someone else. That's the problem!

MARTHA. Yes, that's right! There'll always be someone else – you can't change that!

KURT. We can! We can change it if you help me!

MARTHA. I don't know if I can!

Pause.

KURT. I wanted to be someone you could respect!

KURT *is fighting back tears.*

MARTHA. I do respect you! But I need someone who values our lives, Kurt. Not someone who's just going to throw it all away on me!

MARTHA *picks up her bag, takes her keys and her coat.*

KURT. What are you doing?

MARTHA. I'm going to Edel's house.

KURT. Don't do that please!

MARTHA. I can't even *think* any more! My head feels like it's rammed up inside a concrete block!

KURT. You don't have to think! You just have to stay strong.

MARTHA. I don't know if I can. I don't know if I can be strong, Kurt.

KURT. Then let me be strong for you.

MARTHA. I don't know if you *can* be strong! I don't even know if you're just going mad. Or I am. I wouldn't blame you. Who could survive all this?

KURT. This is our life, Martha! We have to survive it! I love you. I've always loved you. Even before I ever knew you I loved you! I'm not going to let you just walk out that door. If you do that, they've won! They've got us! Give me one week. One more week. Can you do that? (*Pause.*) Can you love me?

MARTHA *looks at him.*

Scene Two

Morning. KURT *is changing into his best suit. The phone is ringing, but* KURT *ignores it.* MARTHA *comes in from the bathroom in her pyjamas, going to the phone.* KURT *looks at her and shakes his head. She pauses. The phone stops ringing.*

KURT. They're wondering where I am.

MARTHA. Do you want some breakfast?

KURT *shakes his head.*

KURT. Did you get any sleep?

MARTHA *shakes her head.*

MARTHA. Did you?

KURT *shakes his head.*

Pause.

Do you want a whiskey?

KURT. I better not.

MARTHA *goes to the press and pours herself a drink of whiskey.*

Do you think I'm a coward, Martha?

MARTHA *shakes her head.*

MARTHA. When I was in school we had a teacher everyone was afraid of. And one day I had to do this presentation in front of the whole class and somehow I managed to spill a bottle of ink on his desk. And he beat me so hard in front of everybody that… I did a wee in my pants. And when I got home, I told my dad and do you know what he did? He slapped me. Because he was afraid you see. He was afraid to go into the school.

KURT. Yeah. Memories. *That's* a memory. (*Pause.*) I better go.

MARTHA. Yeah.

KURT. I'll call you.

MARTHA *nods.* KURT *comes to* MARTHA. *There is a hesitation, then he kisses her on her forehead. She touches his arm.*

Scene Three

A restaurant. MARTHA *sits, self-consciously looking at a menu, distracted by the noise and life around her.* KURT *comes in and joins her.*

KURT. Is this okay?

MARTHA. Yeah. Tell me.

KURT. Well first he starts saying I'm a fucking idiot because I put it where people can swim. So I said, 'But you said it was harmless,' and he goes 'Oh well that's some mistake with the poison – it'll all have dispersed now anyway, so let's not make a big thing out of it.'

MARTHA. What did you say?

KURT. I told him I was going to the police.

MARTHA. Oh God…

KURT. Yeah, and then he went fucking bananas. He started shouting at me, saying I must be off my head, and I drink too much and all this and that he was gonna report *me*! I said, 'Fine you report me and I'll report you and I'll tell the police what I know and you can tell them what you know, alright?' And then I nearly started laughing because he suddenly starts going on that we're all just sausages.

MARTHA. We're all just what?

KURT. Sausages. He says, 'I'm a big sausage. You're only a little sausage. And a big sausage can be in the pan for ages and it won't get burned. But you're only a little sausage, Kurt, you'll be burnt alive in two seconds flat.'

MARTHA. So what did you say?

KURT. I said 'Alright. You're a big sausage. Fine.' And then, I don't know. Something changed. He looks at me and he goes, 'Who have you told about this?' And I don't know why. I just lied, and I said, 'A lot of people.' And suddenly he completely changes and he says, 'Look, your baby is in the hospital, you must be worried out of your mind. Let me make sure he's seeing the right doctors and I'll make sure we get the correct compensation package drawn up, okay? But look, if you go to the police, my hands'll be tied, Kurt, I won't be able to protect you from what the company will want to do. They'll come down on you and you'll be suspended out of your job and they'll sue you and you won't be able to get work, so let's... let's keep talking about this.' And I knew then that he was terrified. I could see him breaking out in a sweat. So I said, 'Alright. Okay.' And I left, and... I went straight to the police.

MARTHA. Oh Kurt...

KURT. Yeah! Then *they* didn't know what to make of me, just walking in and walking up to the desk. They took me into a... a kind of a canteen and they wrote up a report. The guy doing it didn't know what to say. But he told me he didn't think I was gonna get locked up. Or, if I did, it wouldn't be for long time. (*Pause.*) They're gonna check the lake and... go up to the hospital to ask about... Stefan's injuries. (*Long pause.*) That's it.

Scene Four

Evening at the flat. MARTHA *carries a sleeping Stefan into the living room. She places him into his cot. She puts a blanket over him and stands looking down at him.* KURT *comes in from work in his driving clothes.* MARTHA *watches him as he puts his bag and his lunch things away.*

MARTHA. Well?

KURT. New rosters were up. The boss wasn't there.

MARTHA. He'll be busy I'd say!

KURT. I know! (*Pause.*) Well. First day survived, anyway.

MARTHA. Yeah. (*Pause.*) Kurt.

> KURT *turns and looks at her.* MARTHA *looks towards the cot.* KURT *goes over. He looks down at Stefan. He puts his hands to his face, silently overcome.*

Scene Five

At the allotment. It's a warm summer's evening. KURT *is working while Stefan plays around in the muck.* KURT *goes to take a drink.* MARTHA *is miles away.*

KURT. What a day.

MARTHA. Mmm.

KURT. Alright?

> MARTHA *nods.*

MARTHA. Scared, I suppose.

> *Pause.*

KURT. You've got to finish what you start, Martha.

MARTHA. Yeah.

Pause.

KURT. Yeah. (*Short pause.*) I don't know if it's of any use but... (*Pause.*) The union guy came up to me yesterday. I never really spoke to him before, but he said, 'Look, I've been hearing this and I been hearing that, you know?'

MARTHA. Who told him?

KURT. He said they have their channels all up in the management and all this.

MARTHA. Does he know you're not in the union?

KURT. Yeah, I'd say he does.

Pause.

MARTHA. What does he want?

KURT. He says if what we've told the police is true... they might be able to help us. (*Pause.*) He said he could come round on Saturday. Him and some other guy.

Pause.

MARTHA. What did you say?

KURT. I said yeah. Come round.

MARTHA. Do you think that's a good idea?

KURT. I don't know. He said... in the union like... You're not on your own, you know?

MARTHA. You've done pretty good on your own. So far.

KURT. Yeah but... it strengthens your hand. You know?

Pause.

MARTHA. Don't let them talk for you though.

KURT. But that's what they do.

MARTHA. Yeah, but you have to make sure they say what... you... you know. They don't just take it all over now.

Pause.

KURT. I'm just gonna meet them. (*Short pause.*) We're just gonna meet them, Martha.

Pause.

MARTHA. Kurt, look. He's got right into all the beds.

KURT *looks at Stefan, watching him for a few moments.*

KURT. Leave him.

KURT *sits with* MARTHA. *They watch Stefan. Without looking at* KURT, MARTHA *reaches down and takes* KURT*'s hand, the afternoon light turning to dusk, and fading away.*

A Nick Hern Book

This version of *The Nest* first published in Great Britain as a paperback original in 2016 by Nick Hern Books Limited, The Glasshouse, 49a Goldhawk Road, London W12 8QP, in association with the Young Vic Theatre, London, and The Lyric Theatre, Belfast

The Nest copyright © 2016 Conor McPherson
Das Nest copyright © 1975 Franz Xaver Kroetz

Conor McPherson has asserted his right to be identified as the author of this version

Cover design by AKA

Designed and typeset by Nick Hern Books, London
Printed and bound in Great Britain by CPI Group (UK) Ltd

A CIP catalogue record for this book is available from the British Library

ISBN   9781 84842 606 1

www.nickhernbooks.co.uk

facebook.com/nickhernbooks

twitter.com/nickhernbooks